ROCKFORD PUBLIC LIBRARY

3 1112 018098760

W9-BIA-734

WITHDRAWN

J
Ha
Ar

Kid Pick!

Title: _____

Author: _____

Picked by: _____

_____

Why I love this book:

_____

_____

ROCKFORD PUBLIC LIBRARY
Rockford, Illinois
www.rockfordpubliclibrary.org
815-965-9511

ARTIFICIAL INTELLIGENCE

Michael C. Harris

mc **Marshall Cavendish**
Benchmark

ROCKFORD PUBLIC LIBRARY

This edition first published in 2011 in the United States
by Marshall Cavendish Benchmark.

Marshall Cavendish Benchmark
99 White Plains Road
Tarrytown, NY 10591
www.marshallcavendish.us

Copyright © 2011 Q2AMedia

Published by Marshall Cavendish Benchmark
An imprint of Marshall Cavendish Corporation

All rights reserved.

No part of this publication may be reproduced, stored in a retrieval system or transmitted,
in any form or by any means, electronic, mechanical, photocopying, recording, or otherwise,
without the prior permission of the copyright owner. Request for permission should be addressed
to the Publisher, Marshall Cavendish Corporation, 99 White Plains Road, Tarrytown, NY 10591.
Tel: (914) 332-8888, fax: (914) 332-1888.

All Internet sites were available and accurate when this book was sent to press.

This publication represents the opinions and views of the author based on Michael C. Harris's
personal experience, knowledge, and research. The information in this book serves as a general
guide only. The author and publisher have used their best efforts in preparing this book and
disclaim liability rising directly and indirectly from the use and application of this book.

Other Marshall Cavendish Offices:
Marshall Cavendish International (Asia) Private Limited, 1 New Industrial Road, Singapore 536196 • Marshall Cavendish
International (Thailand) Co Ltd. 253 Asoke, 12th Flr, Sukhumvit 21 Road, Klongtoey Nua, Wattana, Bangkok 10110, Thailand •
Marshall Cavendish (Malaysia) Sdn Bhd, Times Subang, Lot 46, Subang Hi-Tech Industrial Park, Batu Tiga, 40000 Shah Alam,
Selangor Darul Ehsan, Malaysia

Marshall Cavendish is a trademark of Times Publishing Limited

Library of Congress Cataloging-in-Publication Data
Harris, Michael C. (Michael Christopher), 1963-
Artificial intelligence / Michael C. Harris.
p. cm. — (Cool science)
Includes index.
ISBN 978-1-60870-076-9
1. Artificial intelligence—Juvenile literature. I. Title.
Q335.4.H37 2011
006.3—dc22
2009053772

Created by Q2AMedia
Series Editor: Bonnie Dobkin
Art Director: Harleen Mehta
Client Service Manager: Santosh Vasudevan
Project Manager: Kumar Kunal
Photo research: Anju Pathak, Debabrata Sen
Designer: Cheena Yadav

The photographs in this book are used by permission and through the courtesy of:

Cover: Brand X Pictures/Photolibrary, Emin Kuliyev/Shutterstock, Zsolt Nyulaszi/Shutterstock
Half title: Apdesign/Shutterstock

4: Andrea Danti/Shutterstock; 5: 2010 American Honda Motor Co. Inc.; 6: Toponium/Shutterstock, Jean-Francois Vermette/
Istockphoto; 7t: Oleksandr Koval/Shutterstock; 7b: 20th Century Fox/The Kobal Collection; 8: Mandy Godbehear/Shutterstock;
9t: Arenacreative/Shutterstock; 9b: ArchMan/Shutterstock; 10t: Yuri Samsonov/Shutterstock; 10cr: The Bridgeman Art Library/
Photolibrary; 10cl: Courtesy of IBM Corporate Archives; 10b: NSA/CSS; 11: James M Phelps, Jr/Shutterstock; 12: www.ilmarefilm.org;
13l: SRI International, Menlo Park, Calif; 13r: Francesco Ridolfi/Shutterstock; 14: Courtesy of IBM Corporate Archives;
15: Andy Freeberg/Hulton Archive/Getty Images; 16: (c) Google Inc. Used with permission; 17: © Google Inc. Used with permission;
18: AP Photo; 19: Walt Disney Pictures/The Kobal Collection; 20: Gene Chutka/Istockphoto; 21t: Michael Buckner/Getty Images;
21b: © 2010 Electronic Arts Inc.; 22: Lucian Coman/Dreamstime; 23: Adela Manea/Dreamstime; 24: Yuri Shchipakin/Shutterstock,
Giraffarte/Istockphoto; 25: © 1996-2010, Amazon.com, Inc.; 26: Dreamstime; 27: Red Dot Studio/Istockphoto; 28: Hendrickson
(US.Army)/National Archives and Records Administration; 29: United States Air Force photo/Lt. Col. Tim Pfeifer; 30t: U.S. Air Force
photo/Lt. Col. Leslie Pratt; 30b: PFC Daniel Klein, USMC/Defense Imagery.Mil; 31: Communication Specialist 2nd Class Gabriel
S. Weber/Army.Mil; 32: Bojan Fatur/Istockphoto; 33: Konstantin Sutyagin/Shutterstock; 34t: ©2005, CE Manley, CUMC/Allen
Pavilion; 34b: © Intuitive Surgical, Inc.; 35: Dima Gavrysh/AP Photo; 36: Izabela Zaremba/Shutterstock; 37: Gene J. Puskar/
AP Photo; 38: Robert Mizerek/Dreamstime; 39: Tlorna/Shutterstock; 40: University of California; 41: David Mack/
Science Photo Library; 42: Ken Andreyo, Carnegie Mellon University; 43: Everett Collection/Rex Features;
44: Frank Capri/Hulton Archive/Getty Images; 45: Solent News/Rex Features

Q2AMedia Art Bank: 16, 23, 24

Printed in Malaysia (T)

1 3 5 6 4 2

CONTENTS

Imagining the Future

We've all seen the movies and read the books. Machines have become intelligent. They run our homes and control our businesses. Sometimes they even try to take over the world!

Science fiction writers and moviemakers have created these fascinating visions of what a future with intelligent machines might be like. Often, they involve robots that look and act like people, or computers that suddenly take on a life of their own. These images are exciting, but sometimes pretty scary.

Over the past several decades, though, scientists and inventors have developed their own version of a world full of intelligent machines. These scientists work in a branch of computer science called artificial intelligence, or AI. Simply put, artificial intelligence is the science of creating machines to solve problems and do work that is too complicated for the human brain to do by itself. It has been changing our world in exciting and amazing ways.

Some of these developments are what you might have imagined: planes that fly without pilots, robots that help perform operations. But other examples of artificial intelligence are so common and familiar that you might not even notice them. The computer you use every day? The satellite TV some people watch? The smartphones that everybody wants? The latest gaming console? They are all examples of artificial intelligence in action.

A version of ASIMO will someday assist people in their homes.

WHAT IS ARTIFICIAL INTELLIGENCE?

So what exactly is artificial intelligence? Is it the same kind of intelligence that people have? The answer is yes . . . and no.

Defining Artificial Intelligence

Artificial intelligence is very complex, so a good place to start is with a simple definition. Artificial intelligence is the science of making intelligent machines that perform tasks as well as, or better and faster than, humans can. Artificial intelligence isn't really about intelligence, though. It's about solving problems. But the solutions in artificial intelligence are always math- and computer-based.

For example, think of a calculator. You can punch in a bunch of large numbers and the calculator will be able to add them together as fast as you can enter them. You could add them all up with a paper and pencil, but the calculator can do the "thinking" much faster than you can. Would you say the calculator is intelligent? No. But can it do some of the same things your own brain can? Definitely. Plus, it can do those things much more quickly and accurately.

The speed of a handheld calculator is impressive, but top supercomputers can perform 1,000 trillion operations per second!

The Birth of a Science

When and how did artificial intelligence begin? Until the 1950s, the phrase itself didn't even exist! But that changed thanks to John McCarthy, the "Father of Artificial Intelligence."

John McCarthy is a mathematician who believes that machines can be made to reason like humans. In 1956, he sponsored the Dartmouth Summer Research Project on Artificial Intelligence to explore that possibility. For the conference, McCarthy brought together some of the most creative thinkers in mathematics, logic, **engineering**, **psychology**, and the then new field of computer science. As a result of this conference, artificial intelligence became recognized as a separate field of study.

McCarthy, now eighty-two, has long thought that computers and artificial intelligence could change the way people live and societies function. Decades ago, McCarthy suggested that computing services would become something like electricity—they would be wired into every house. Though he didn't foresee wireless computing, McCarthy seems to have been proven right!

ARTIFICIAL INTELLIGENCE IN THE MOVIES

In the 1951 film *The Day The Earth Stood Still*, an alien named Klaatu comes to Earth to warn people to stop fighting wars. He brings Gort, a large robot that has been programmed to disarm guns and weapons—and to destroy Earth if its citizens won't change their ways. When the movie came out, people were just learning about the amazing things computers could do. The futuristic Gort fascinated and terrified them.

A VERY OLD IDEA

For thousands of years, scientists have been trying to understand how human beings think. They have also searched for ways to help people think better and faster.

Early Ideas

You could say the history of artificial intelligence dates as far back as 350 BCE. Greek **philosopher** Aristotle wrote about a system of logic, or the science of thinking, that influenced scientists and philosophers for years to come.

You can think of logic as a system for making decisions and solving problems. Simply put, this system depends on a series of questions or statements. Based on these statements, we draw conclusions or decide on next steps. Here's a simple example of how you might make a decision.

Should I watch the football game on TV or go to the stadium?

If the football game starts early, then I will watch it at home.

If the game starts later, then I will go to the stadium.

The game starts at 3:00. **Therefore,** I will go to the stadium.

Computers mimic this same kind of thinking. All of the information they work with has been programmed into their systems in terms of *yes/no, true/false, if/then, on/off,* or *1 or 0.* The information is also provided in countless variations. For instance, in the football example, an option could have been this: IF the game starts later AND the weather is pleasant AND we're playing a good team, THEN I'll go to the stadium OR I'll go to a friend's house.

No matter how complex artificial intelligence systems get, information must be programmed in at this basic level, and with every possible variation. You can imagine why computer codes are really, really long. Some take months or years to write. But when they are finished, some computers can complete hundreds of thousands of tasks in as little as one second.

	A	B	C	D	E	F
1						
2	Start time	End time	Sum			
3	10,75	12,50	1,75			
4	9,25	10,25	1			
5	18,00	19,00	1			
6	9,25	10,25	1			
7	14,50	16,50	2			
8	8,75	9.25	0,5			
9	21,75	22,25	0,5			
10	11,75	12,75	1			
11	22,50	23,50	1			
12						
13						
14						
15						
16						
17						
18						
19						

EARLY "THINKING" MACHINES

Pascal's Helpful Gadget

Blaise Pascal was a whiz kid. In 1642, at the age of nineteen, Pascal invented and built the first known calculating machine that could add and subtract. He built it to help his father do his tax collection work. The Pascaline, as the machine was called, can be considered the first step toward what would become the modern-day computing machine.

The First Calculator?

In the late 1800s, British mathematician and inventor Charles Babbage designed what he called a "Difference Engine." It was intended to do very complicated math problems. Babbage never actually built the machine, but in 1991, the Science Museum in London decided to see if his invention would have worked. They built it following Babbage's directions, and it worked exactly as planned!

Turing's Revolutionary Machine

In the 1930s, Britain's Alan Turing came up with a model for a machine that could solve complex problems through a series of simple steps. Machines based on this model were called Turing machines. These devices seem simple now, but they were really the earliest form of the modern computer.

Making Machines Think

For thousands of years, scientists and philosophers have been trying to understand how people think. They have also searched for ways to help us think better and faster.

It's All About Algorithms

Computers don't really think like we do. But they are extremely good at following specific directions, called algorithms. An algorithm is a step-by-step set of instructions that solves a problem or completes a task. For example, here is the algorithm you might follow if you were trying to figure out why a lamp didn't work.

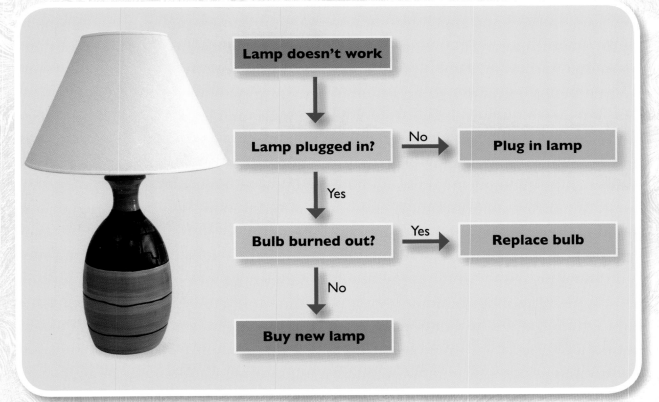

Think of algorithms as similar to directions for building a model. If you follow all the directions exactly, you'll end up with a model that looks the way it was meant to. If there is an error in the directions, or you skip a step, your model won't turn out as it should. Similarly, when computers follow a well-constructed algorithm, they are able to complete the task they're asked to do. If there's an error in the programming, however, the computer will appear to have made a mistake.

ELIZA Speaks

One of the most impressive early successes in artificial intelligence was ELIZA. ELIZA was a computer program invented by Joseph Weizenbaum, a professor of computer science at MIT. Invented in 1966, ELIZA was able to respond to information that was entered into the computer.

Joseph Weizenbaum demonstrates ELIZA's abilities by typing in a question.

ELIZA's responses were fairly basic. They were like those a doctor or psychologist would use when gathering information. For example, if someone typed in "My head hurts," ELIZA would respond, "Why does your head hurt?" ELIZA's responses were always questions, but this proved to other computer scientists that they could create more complicated forms of artificial intelligence.

Shakey the Robot

Called the "first electronic person," Shakey the Robot was created at Stanford University between 1966 and 1972. The robot had an antenna, a camera, a computer board, and wheels. A **programmer** would type a command into a machine that would transmit the directions to Shakey. But Shakey could also solve problems on its own.

In one experiment, Shakey was commanded to move a large, heavy block from one place to another. Then someone came in and pushed the block away from Shakey. The robot was able to adjust its actions to find the block again and keep pushing. This was an important development in artificial intelligence. It meant machines could be programmed to reason, or think in a logical way. Scientists continued to expand on this knowledge to make machines that could think in more and more advanced ways.

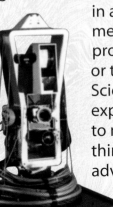

Shakey was not elegant. It was simply a box of electronics on wheels, with bump detectors at the base and a TV camera and range finder for a head.

INSIDE KNOWLEDGE

Early artificial intelligence programmers thought the complicated game of chess was a great way to judge how intelligent a computer could be. As hard as they tried, though, they couldn't create a machine that could beat human players.

Then, in 1989, the IBM computer Deep Thought beat chess master David Levy. How? It could analyze two million chess positions per move in tournament games! In 1997, world chess champion Garry Kasparov lost an entire match to Deep Blue, IBM's follow-up to Deep Thought. Today, you can play with your own PC—and you'll usually lose!

THE COMPUTER REVOLUTION

The computer is probably the most important technology invented by humans since the printing press in the fifteenth century. In only a few decades, most of the world has come to depend on computer technology for almost everything.

This 1953 computer was the IBM 701. It performed thirty-three different kinds of operations.

A Big, Slow Start

It's hard to say when the very first computer was created. In World War II, though, the armies of Britain, Germany, and the United States all had working computers. These weren't like the computers we have today. America's Electronic Numerical Integrator and Computer (ENIAC) weighed thirty tons, took up an entire basement, and used 17,000 **vacuum tubes** to handle the electricity.

JUST AMAZING

Ever wonder how fast modern computers are? In 2008, an American supercomputer named Roadrunner, built by IBM in its Los Alamos laboratory in New Mexico, was able to complete 1,000 trillion operations in just one second!

In the 1950s, IBM made computers for business use. These were much smaller than the military computers—they only took up part of a room. Twenty years later, computers began to look like the ones we now use, though still much bigger. More and more businesses began to use them. By the late 1980s, not only were businesses using computers, but nearly 20 percent of U.S. homes also contained at least one personal computer. Artificial intelligence was suddenly available in spare rooms and home offices around the country.

GENIUS AT WORK

In the mid-1970s, two college-age kids—Bill Gates and Steve Jobs—changed the course of computer history. Gates started the company Microsoft, which teamed with IBM to make software for desktop computers. Jobs cofounded Apple Computers with his partner Steve Wozniak and created an **operating system** that made it very easy for people to use a computer. The genius of these men, combined with a desktop-sized system created by a company called Micro Instrumentation Telemetry Systems, began what is now called the **computer revolution**. Computers became a part of everyday life.

Steve Jobs (left) and Bill Gates changed society when—as young men—they created computers and operating systems that people could use in their homes and at school.

The Internet Changed Everything

The Internet began in 1969. At that time, it was simply a phone line connection between three computers in three different cities. It was created for the Defense Advanced Research Projects Agency (DARPA), a research group for the U.S. military. The system was called ARPANET (Advanced Research Projects Agency Network).

Eventually, industries other than the military started creating similar computer-based communication systems. By the late 1980s, many worldwide systems had joined together to create the worldwide web (the www in most Internet addresses), which is what we now call the Internet.

Smart Searching

The wealth of information on the Internet is only useful if we can find it. That's where search engines come in. And what makes search engines work? Algorithms, of course!

In 1998, Larry Page (left) and Sergey Brin (right) decided to organize the world's online information—and created Google.

When you search for something on the Internet, you type the words into a user **interface** page. It takes your words and uses them in an algorithm that matches them with what you're looking for. This action is a kind of artificial intelligence called *natural language processing*. When the item is found, headlines and a snippet of the material are posted in a results page.

Web   Images   Maps   News   Shopping   Gmail   more ▼

Google | google | Search | Advanced Search / Preferences

Web   News   10 of about 2,760,000,000

Related searches: google phone

News results for google
Review: Google's HTC Dream phone   That's it? - 46 minutes ago
By Bonnie Cha and Nicole Lee (CNET) – it's been a little more than a year since
Google Android was announced and rumors of a little device called the HTC ...
The Age   CNN - 701 related articles »
Google Earth Lands On Apple's iPhone - InformationWeek - 108 related articles »
Debunking Google's security vulnerability disclosure propaganda -
CNET News - 44 related articles »

Try a Goo
Personalize
your favori
www.goog

Google
Enables users to search the Web, Usenet, and images Features include PageRank, caching
and translation of results, and an option to find similar pages.   Show stock quote for GOOG
www.google.com/- 7k- Cached - Similar pages

Today, in addition to its search functions, Google provides a wide range of business services.

Google Takes Over

Who hasn't used Google? This search engine has become so popular that its name has become a verb: you google people or places when you want to learn more about them.

Larry Page and Sergey Brin created the search engine Google in their college dorm room at Stanford University. Their mission was "to organize the world's information and make it universally accessible and useful."

What made Google unique was that it looked for relationships between websites rather than only looking for the search words. Google launched in 1998 and quickly became the number one search engine in the world.

Just Amazing

How much do we depend on the Internet today? Here are some statistics.

- Google estimates it handles more than 300 million searches a day.
- Approximately 247 billion e-mails are sent every day.
- 71 percent of all Internet users have bought something online.
- Trillions of dollars are transferred over the Internet every day worldwide in banking, business, and personal transactions.

ENTERTAINMENT

Some of the most innovative uses of artificial intelligence have been in the entertainment field. In return, systems created for games and movies have done a lot to advance the entire field of artificial intelligence!

All Work and No Play?

Gaming has been a part of artificial intelligence from the very beginning of computers. But the kind of gaming we think of today really kicked off in the 1970s with Pong, a simple tennis-like game. More games—Galaga, Donkey Kong, Pac-Man— quickly followed. All used some form of artificial intelligence algorithm programming. Over the years, games became more complex, and in-home gaming units became available. A multibillion-dollar industry was born.

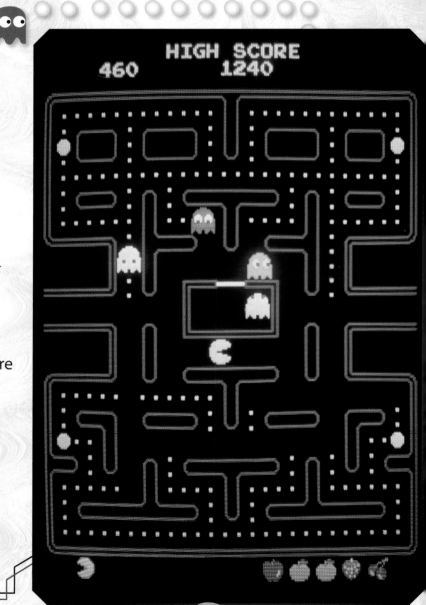

HIGH SCORE
460   1240

Pac-Man was released in 1980 but is still played today. It is considered one of the great classic video games.

Computer-Generated Imagery

At the same time gaming was expanding the uses of artificial intelligence, moviemakers were learning to create some amazing special effects using artificial intelligence algorithms. Computer-generated imagery (CGI) allows filmmakers to create any kind of background, special effect, or character they want.

Animators, for example, begin the process by creating character "frames." Then, computer algorithms let them add realistic color, shadow, texture, and movement. Hollywood and the gaming industry worked to take artificial intelligence in new, creative directions. Their work helped to advance artificial intelligence as much as that of scientists and engineers.

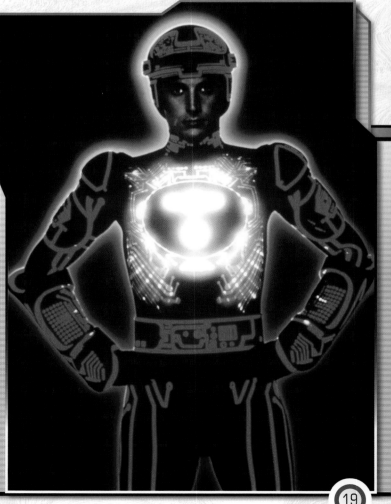

ARTIFICIAL INTELLIGENCE IN THE MOVIES

Tron was a movie and video arcade game that changed the way both industries used artificial intelligence algorithms. The 1982 movie followed human characters who get pulled into the mainframe of a video game. The movie used more CGI than any other movie had before, creating a unique look on the big screen. The same was true of the *Tron* game, which had images that looked almost three-dimensional. Soon all the game companies were trying to make games that looked like *Tron*.

How Interactive Games Work

What makes some computer games interactive? They depend on something called fuzzy logic. Most artificial intelligence applications use simple and direct programming logic, or directions, the *yes/no* or *if/then* approach. A certain action has a specific result.

Fuzzy logic programming is not that direct. Many different combinations are possible, including "if this happens, MAYBE that happens." Or, if the character does something close to one action, then a particular result will occur. For example, in a *Mario Bros.* game, when Mario kicks a Shellcreeper, fuzzy logic allows Mario's foot to kick anywhere close to the Shellcreeper to flip it over.

Living *IN* a Game?

Interactive games have become so advanced that players have the ability to simulate real life. That is, they can create a virtual life in a virtual world. *The Sims* is a series of life **simulation** games in which players create characters and are in charge of taking care of them. Eating, going to work, cleaning the house—the player makes all the decisions and controls the actions of the characters.

The artificial intelligence programming behind a game like *The Sims* is all fuzzy logic. For example, if you haven't fed your Sim in a long time, it will act like it's hungry or getting sick. There isn't a yes or no answer to the problem. You have to figure out what the Sim needs to feel better.

GENIUS AT WORK

Will Wright created *The Sims* in the 1990s after his home burned down in a fire. While trying to rebuild his life and create a new home, he was inspired to create a game in which players could do something similar. *The Sims* became the most popular computer game ever.

In this *Sims* game, the player's characters live in a futuristic apartment.

COMMERCIAL AND BUSINESS USES

Today we get cash from machines and buy products from websites. Even multibillion-dollar business deals are made online. What makes all this possible? Artificial intelligence.

Instant Money

Automatic teller machines, or ATMs, are actually simple artificial intelligence devices. The program makes sure your account has money, gives you cash, and deducts the amount from your account. It also let's you deposit money and transfer funds, and can show you your banking history at the push of a button.

Artificial Intelligence is also used by banks and businesses to handle far more complicated financial tasks. For example, credit card companies use artificial intelligence to fight credit card fraud. Complex programs monitor how each card is used. If there is any activity on the card that doesn't "seem right," credit card companies can contact the cardholder to make sure no one else is using the card.

An ATM user activates the machine by inserting a card with a magnetic strip. A unique PIN—personal identification number—keeps the transaction private.

Imitating the Brain

The secret to advanced systems like the one for stopping credit card fraud is called artificial neural networks (ANNs). This is one of the most complicated areas of artificial intelligence. It is also one of the most powerful. ANNs are programs designed to search for patterns of behavior. Early artificial intelligence dealt mainly with yes-or-no questions; ANNs deal with what actions mean and how to organize them.

An artificial neural network takes different types of input, combines them in a variety of ways, and draws conclusions about each combination. It then creates reports of the analyses, called the output.

INSIDE KNOWLEDGE

Almost everyone knows Walmart—it has about six thousand stores worldwide. One of the secrets to its success is its use of artificial neural networks (ANNs). ANNs constantly update what is and isn't selling, and notice what needs to be ordered. So if an ANN finds that stores in Wichita, Kansas, are selling lots of blue-striped running shoes, the program automatically orders more of them to be sent to the Wichita stores. Talk about customer service!

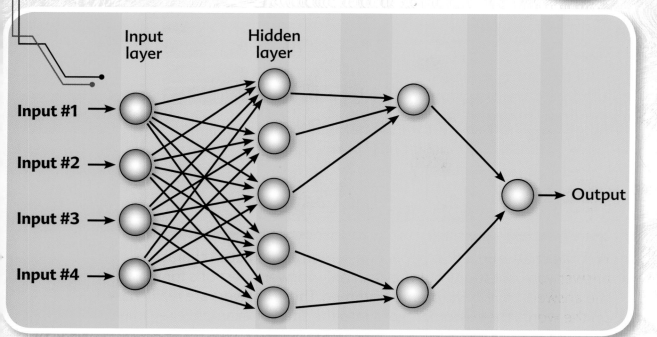

Input layer

Hidden layer

Input #1 →

Input #2 →

Input #3 →

Input #4 →

→ Output

The E-Commerce Explosion

In the mid-1990s, businesses realized that the Internet could be a great new way to reach people and cut costs. First, online stores don't have to keep their shelves stocked with products the way a physical store does. Also, online stores can use artificial intelligence to run their businesses.

For many businesses, hiring people to handle customer requests is too expensive. Instead, they use either **automated** voice systems, or they use chatterbots. Interactive Voice Response systems, or IVRs, allow incoming callers the option of dialing an extension directly, rather than talking to a receptionist. Or, they gather information and send the caller to the right person.

A chatterbot gives users the illusion that they are talking to a person or character.

Website chatterbots that appear on-screen as animated characters answer your questions but they can only answer questions for which the answers have been preprogrammed. These answers are really based on the words the customer types into the site. For example, they may be programmed to recognize a product or service name and then offer options that match the request.

Shopping Online

The shopping habits of American consumers are changing, too. Today, shoppers often purchase products with the click of a mouse instead of a trip to the store. A 2009 report by the U.S. Census Bureau stated that retail e-commerce had reached $127 billion in 2007. The top merchandise categories for percentage of online sales were for books, music, electronics, and appliances.

Amazon.com proved that e-commerce could be a highly profitable way of doing business.

100 greatest **Debut Albums**
of all time
▶ Shop now at Amazon MP3

amazon MP3
Music Downloads for Any Device

Downloads instantly to:
🎵 iTunes Library
⊙ Windows Media Player

MP3 Daily Deal
Today's special: Jason Aldean's brand-new *Wide Open*, available exclusively at Amazon MP3 a day before you'll find it anywhere else. Everyday low price: $9.99
Today's price: $3.99

What's Happening at Amazon MP3

$7.99 Editors' Picks
Ray Guns Are Not Just the Future, the Bird and the Bee: $7.99
Blue Train, John Coltrane: $7.99
Quintana Roo, RH+: $7.99
▶ More $7.99 albums

$6.99 Bob Dylan Albums
Blonde on Blonde: $6.99
Highway 61 Revisited: $6.99
The Freewheelin' Bob Dylan: $6.99
▶ More by Bob Dylan

Free Music
"Mas Fuerte," CuCu Diamantes: $0.00
"Blanket" (Amazon MP3 Exclusive), Jeff Beck (feat. Imogen Heap): $0.00
"Pulling on a Line," Great Lake Swimmers: $0.00
▶ More free music

100 greatest **Indie Rock Albums**
▶ Shop now

The 100 Greatest Indie Rock Albums
Bee Thousand, Guided by Voices: $9.99
In the Aeroplane Over the Sea, Neutral Milk Hotel: $9.99
Spiderland, Slint: $9.99
▶ See all 100 greatest indie rock albums

Browse MP3s
Most Popular
100 Greatest Indie Rock Albums of All Time
American Idol® Originals
ChordStrike Music Blog
Free Songs & Special Deals
MP3 Albums by Price
$4.99 and Under
$5.00 to $5.99
$6.00 to $6.99
$7.00 to $7.99
$8.00 to $8.99
Genres
Alternative & Indie Rock
Blues
Broadway & Vocalists
Children's Music
Christian & Gospel
Classic Rock
Classical: Instrumental
Classical: Opera & Vocal
Comedy & Miscellaneous
Country
Dance & Electronic
Folk
Hard Rock & Metal
Jazz
Latin Music
New Age
Pop
R&B
Rap & Hip-Hop
Rock

New and Notable MP3s   Page 1 of 4

Defying Gravity MP3 Download ~ Keith Urban
$8.99

R.O.O.T.S. [Explicit] MP3 Download ~ Flo Rida
$8.99

NOW 30 MP3 Download ~ Various Artists
$9.49

The Soundstage Sessions MP3 Download ~ Stevie Nicks
$8.99

Quiet Nights MP3 Download ~ Diana Krall
$8.99

Today's Top MP3 Songs
1. Boom Boom Pow by Black Eyed Peas
2. Poker Face by Lady GaGa
3. Right Round by Flo Rida
4. Just Dance by Lady GaGa
5. Gives You Hell by The All-American Rejects
6. Love Story by Taylor Swift
7. The Climb by Miley Cyrus
8. Kiss Me Thru The Phone by Soulja Boy Tell'em
9. You Found Me by The Fray
10. My Life Would Suck Without You by Kelly Clarkson
11. Careless Whisper (single) by Seether
12. Dead And Gone [Feat. Justin... by T.I.
13. Hot N Cold by Katy Perry

Today's Top MP3 Artists
1. The Roots
2. Bat For Lashes
3. Keith Urban
4. Neko Case
5. Flo Rida
6. 99 Perfectly Relaxing Songs
7. Lady GaGa
8. Bob Dylan
9. U2
10. Twilight Soundtrack
11. Carter Burwell
12. The Decemberists
13. Taylor Swift

GENIUS AT WORK

Amazon.com's Jeff Bezos is a science geek who likes to take risks. When he founded what was then solely an online bookstore in 1994, Bezos knew he'd lose money for the first five years. He was right. But by year six, the company started to make money. In 2008, Amazon brought in nearly $20 billion in sales!

ARTIFICIAL INTELLIGENCE AND TRANSPORTATION

Computers and artificial intelligence have made just about everything in our world move faster. So how have they changed the things that were already designed to move quickly, like cars and airplanes and trains?

On Land

Thanks to artificial intelligence, cars now have complicated computer systems for monitoring everything from the temperature in the car to the flow of gas into the engine. In addition, the global positioning system (GPS) devices used by many drivers in the United States provide maps and spoken directions to the driver's destination by collecting information from twenty-four satellites that currently orbit Earth. Similar systems allow security companies to track a driver's location and provide help when needed.

Train systems rely on artificial intelligence programming as well. In many cities, computers schedule and monitor the trains.

Artificial intelligence systems not only provide a driver with directions, they can also track the flow of traffic and adjust routes accordingly.

If the program sees that two trains are getting too close to one another on the same track, one train will be flagged to slow down. In places where high-speed trains are used, artificial intelligence has been used to design the rail system and to monitor all the trains on the track. Although people are still needed to monitor these systems, artificial intelligence monitors trains more quickly and accurately than most people could.

In the Air

Airlines have been using artificial intelligence to help control air traffic for many years. Programs are able to take the information from air traffic radar systems and create a model of what the airspace looks like at any given time. This helps the air traffic controllers, the people who make decisions about when planes can land and take off. If the automated computer system senses a dangerous situation, it alerts the controllers immediately.

Most high-speed trains travel at a rate of 90 to 115 miles (145 to 185 kilometers) per hour.

ARTIFICIAL INTELLIGENCE AND THE MILITARY

The Internet is not the only form of artificial intelligence that has been funded by the U.S. military. Over the years, armies have developed artificial intelligence technology for many purposes.

When the United States entered World War II, military experts felt the country was not well prepared to defend itself or attack its enemies. Soldiers needed a computer to help them calculate the weapon settings needed to ensure the greatest accuracy under different conditions.

The result was ENIAC. This huge computer was one thousand times faster than any other computer that had been built. It was first used to help design the hydrogen bomb. Later, ENIAC was used in gunnery calculations.

Another early project of the DARPA was a system designed to defend the United States against incoming missiles. The system could sense any airborne object entering U.S. airspace. If the object wasn't part of the U.S. military, soldiers could shoot it out of the sky before it reached land.

Computers provided the settings needed to aim this gun accurately.

Artificial intelligence allows guided missiles to follow their targets and adjust direction as necessary.

Controlling Firepower

DARPA also came up with the first guided missile systems. At first, these systems helped soldiers aim bombs more precisely. Later, DARPA created missile systems that allowed soldiers to change the direction of missiles while they were in the air. Finally, even more advanced systems allowed the missiles themselves to change their direction in midair to follow a heat source, like an enemy plane or a tank rolling down a road.

ARTIFICIAL INTELLIGENCE IN THE MOVIES

The 1983 movie *War Games* played on human fears about technology and nuclear war. A teenage hacker accidentally gets into a U.S. military computer system and sets off a nuclear war simulation that nearly starts World War III. The U.S. military really did use computers like the one in the movie to make predictions about missile strikes and potential attacks. *War Games* made the general public more aware of potential threats to the country's security.

Artificial intelligence and remote control devices allow this predator drone to fly into enemy territory without a pilot.

Robots Go to War

Some of the U.S. military's most amazing uses of artificial intelligence involve robots. One impressive example is the armed predator drone. It's an airplane that flies by remote control over enemy air space. Drones are very hard to detect on radar, so they can sneak over areas without being seen. The drones can take pictures and video, then send the images back to the commanders for analysis. The drones can also be armed and sent to destroy enemy targets.

The U.S. military has also developed robots that can be used for many kinds of ground missions. These robots can take pictures and video and then send them back to command. They can identify and disarm land mines. They can even be equipped with weapons or bombs.

This Remote Ordnance Neutralization System (RONS) can survey dangerous areas and carry away hazardous materials.

A Robot Army?

Robot soldiers don't exist yet, but parts of them do. The U.S. military has experimented with exoskeletons, or mechanical body armor. Robotic arms and legs have been developed to help soldiers carry heavy weapons and supplies, and to keep them from getting tired on the battlefield. Using artificial intelligence, these skeletons are able to respond to the weight of a backpack or the added strain of an uphill climb and give soldiers the extra help they need.

Inside Knowledge

Called the Big Dog, this odd remote-controlled robot can be used to carry supplies onto the battlefield. It is designed to be able to walk over any **terrain**, including mountains. The hardest parts of the design are the legs and the knees. When we walk over bumpy ground our feet and knees react instantly to keep our balance. Imagine how difficult it was to program an artificial intelligence system to do that!

ARTIFICIALLY INTELLIGENT DOCTOR?

Every profession can benefit from the power of artificial intelligence. Even the practice of medicine has been revolutionized by new systems.

Artificial intelligence is becoming more and more crucial in medicine today. It can complete or assist with a wide variety of tasks. For example, artificial intellegence helps doctors and other health practitioners figure out what's wrong with people by analyzing images and data. It directs the movement of artificial limbs. Artificial intelligence even helps doctors perform surgeries!

Magnetic resonance imaging (MRI) is used to create images of the inside of the body. Artificial intelligence programs may be used to help doctors analyze those images.

Artificial intelligence programs can be used to help doctors detect abnormalities in diagnostic scans.

Keeping Us Healthy

Doctors use ANNs—the programs that look for patterns in large amounts of data—to help with diagnosing, or identifying, what's wrong with patients. How does this work? A doctor enters information about the patient into the program. The program organizes that information and compares it to what's in its **database**. It then presents the doctor or medical team with a number of likely diagnoses to consider and evaluate.

Artificial intelligence programs help doctors in other ways, too. Some programs can look at X rays and other medical images and create reports listing what they "see." In hospitals, nurses depend on artificial intelligence programs to watch over patients. All those machines that are hooked up to a patient in a hospital? Nearly every one uses some type of artificial intelligence system to monitor what's going on and alert staff to any problems or irregularities.

GENIUS AT WORK

Cancer is one of the most common and most deadly diseases. What if there were a way to diagnose it early on? Researchers at the University of Chicago have designed an artificial intelligence program that analyzes medical images. It is far superior to other methods in helping doctors determine whether a person's cancer has metastasized, or spread. When doctors detect the cancer at its earliest stages, the odds of a patient surviving increase greatly. This kind of use of artificial intelligence is truly life saving.

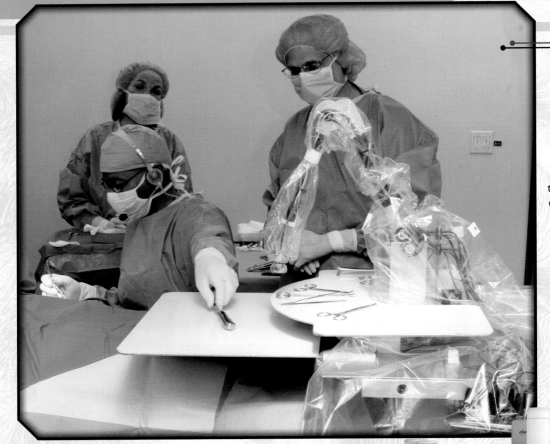

By handling the instruments, the robot Penelope allows the nurses to help with more complicated tasks.

"Paging Doctor Robot. Paging Doctor Robot."

Some doctors are using a robot to assist them during surgery. Named Penelope, this robot—actually, a robotic arm—is similar to those used on automobile assembly lines. Penelope is voice activated. This means the doctor can simply say "sponge" or "scalpel" and the robotic arm finds one and gently hands it over. Penelope also keeps track of every item that has been used during the operation. These robots help extend a hospital's staff, and also reduce the chance of human error.

What about robot doctors actually performing surgery? It's happening already. The da Vinci Surgical System looks a little like a metal spider with multiple robotic arms. It has many different attachments, or "hands." The tools a surgeon uses are simply attached to the hands as needed. The da Vinci system and similar robots have been used on surgeries as complicated as heart bypass and liver transplants.

Of course, this robotic surgeon doesn't know what to do without instruction from a human surgeon. That's where artificial intelligence comes in. The surgeon sits in another part of the operating room in front of a computer console and looks through a three-dimensional (3-D) camera system. Then he or she tells the robot what to do, using hand controls that are a little like joysticks for computer games. Why use robotic arms at all? Because robots make fewer mistakes, they're more precise when making delicate cuts, and they reduce the risk of infection.

Like the Real Thing

Artificial intelligence also has allowed great advances in prosthetic limbs. Once, patients had to make an artificial limb move through muscle power, and the movement could be awkward and uncomfortable. Today, artificial intelligence can take over much of the work by reading nerve impulses sent from the person's brain. The limb moves almost as naturally as a real arm or leg.

INSIDE KNOWLEDGE

With the help of microchips—tiny computer hardware parts—bionic limbs have become more advanced than ever. The Power Knee is a computer-based artificial leg in which a computer is built into the knee. Using artificial intelligence, the Power Knee responds to signals from the nerve endings at the end of the person's thigh. Instead of the user having to "pull" the artificial leg along when walking, the Power Knee automatically keeps pace.

Smart Security

Artificial intelligence technology has been used for many types of security systems—home and business, computers, and national security. Because the systems can think faster and respond more quickly than humans, they make ideal security systems.

Protecting Our Stuff

The security systems that people use in their homes make use of very basic computing functions to monitor doors and windows and detect movement. Museums and military research centers use more advanced artificial intelligence systems to protect their treasures and sensitive data. **Sensors** placed throughout a facility keep a constant read on the airflow or temperature in a room. If those readings change even a little bit when no one is supposed to be in the room, the security system sounds an alert.

This high-end surveillance room uses a variety of cameras and sensors to monitor activity in an entire building.

Computer Security

Websites and businesses spend millions of dollars every year keeping themselves safe from computer hackers—people who try to break into other people's computer systems, or use them in ways that weren't intended.

One of the most important computer security inventions the past decade is CAPTCHA. CAPTCHA is a program that enables websites to protect themselves from other computer programs—for example, programs designed to enter a ticket-buying site and scoop up all the best seats. The letters and numbers in the CAPTCHA images are purposely hard to read. This is done so only a real person can figure out what they are. Artificial intelligence is used to create these CAPTCHA images and confirm when someone gets it right. The program has been very successful: 200 million of these images are created every day.

CAPTCHA images cannot be interpreted by scanning machines because each one is unique.

A few years after creating CAPTCHA, Luis Von Ahn created reCAPTCHA. reCAPTCHA is presently being used to help put over 110 years of the *New York Times* newspaper online.

These old newspapers are being scanned by computers so that they can be put online. But the scanners can't read all the words and letters correctly. So, along with a CAPTCHA security code, web users are also shown a small chunk of confusing text from the *Times*. Von Ahn figured that if people can figure out a CAPTCHA security code, they can probably figure out the blurred or confusing newspaper text as well. He was right!

SECURITY CHECK

Type the characters you see in the picture below.

Can't read this? Try another.

enertioc

Luis von Ahn created CAPTCHA when he was only twenty-one years old.

Scanning
Finger Print

.....SCAN COMPLETED

Your Biometric Identity

Our faces, voices, and fingerprints are all unique. Security systems use biometrics—the science of analyzing biological data—to make use of this fact. Fingerprinting has been around for a long time. But with artificial intelligence programming, a sensor can immediately read a person's fingerprint and make decisions about that individual. For example, Walt Disney World uses fingerprinting machines at its entrances to make sure that only one person uses a particular ticket.

Our voices and faces are also unique forms of identification. Biometric artificial intelligence programs are able to scan a person's face or voice and identify unique characteristics to create an identity code. When that person speaks or looks into a security camera, the program scans the voice or face and looks for a match in the security system. No match means no entry.

Scanners can read a person's fingerprint and compare it to prints in a database. If there's a match, the computer knows the person has been cleared by security.

The Eyes Have It

The biometric system that has been most successful is eye recognition. The artificial intelligence program takes a picture of the iris, or colored part of your eye. It then creates a coded identity that is 100 percent unique for every person. This kind of identification security works well because the eye doesn't wear down like fingerprints or change like voice.

A person's iris is as unique as a fingerprint and can be used for identification.

INSIDE KNOWLEDGE

After the terrorist attacks of September 11, 2001, the U.S. government put into place the US-VISIT program. All people from other countries who want to come into the United States must have their fingerprint scanned and a digital photo taken at the airport. Artificial intelligence checks the scanned information against government databases. Officials can immediately see if a person is a known terrorist or criminal.

SEARCHING

THE FUTURE OF ARTIFICIAL INTELLIGENCE

Computer technology is getting faster and smaller and more advanced every day. So what should we look for in the future? Expect some pretty amazing stuff!

Imagine a powerful little computer that's as small as a particle of dust. Artificial intelligence scientists have imagined it. It's called Smart Dust. Smart Dust could be scattered inside a hospital to monitor the air temperature at all times. It could be used to sense vibrations on the ground to warn about earthquakes. The military could use it to secretly monitor the enemy's movements. When artificial intelligence robots get this small, there's no telling what they might be able to do!

Smart Dust chips are made from silicon. They are shown here on a drop of oil.

Now think about this. What if we could send tiny robots into our bodies to fight off diseases or repair a damaged organ? That's what nanobots may be able to do one day. Nanobots are tiny robots that are programmed to perform very specific tasks. They can also be programmed to follow wireless commands from doctors. Experiments are going on to make nanobots from human DNA. They would be injected right into people's veins and do whatever the programmer has told them to do, from cleaning out an artery to destroying diseased cells.

Just Amazing

What if the human brain could be "computerized"? We're not there yet, but BrainGate is an incredible start. A tiny computer interface is implanted in a person's brain and connected directly to a computer. Complex artificial intelligence programming translates brain waves into algorithm commands that tell the computer what to do. BrainGate was designed to help paralyzed or partially paralyzed people do things such as read e-mail, turn on lights, and even move motorized wheelchairs.

Nanobots the size of blood cells could be used to fight heart disease.

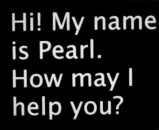

Hi! My name is Pearl. How may I help you?

Carnegie Mellon

In-Home Robot Help

As long as there has been science fiction, there have been robots in human form. They were shown cleaning houses, preparing meals, working in factories, and going to war. They have even been best friends, protectors, and companions.

Now these robots are really entering our lives, and for very practical reasons. By 2020, the number of people in America over the age of sixty-five will have nearly doubled since 1990. Who will take care of this large elderly population? Artificial intelligence scientists are working on a solution called Seniorbots.

Seniorbots are robotic caregivers. They would be programmed to do such things as remind seniors to take their medication, and to act as an alert system in case of a medical emergency. But they could do everyday things to help as well, like reach things that are too high for a senior to reach. They could even open cans and jars!

Pearl the NurseBot is already doing some of these things. She's designed to communicate via a touch screen with senior citizens. She can also help doctors do remote checkups on elderly patients. As Pearl's designers have said, "We have succeeded in helping people live longer. Now we need to help them live better."

The expression on Pearl's face was carefully designed so that users would be comfortable having her around.

Are Cyborgs for Real?

Cyborgs—beings that are part human and part robot—are just ideas from science fiction stories, right?

Not exactly. Today we use artificial intelligence robotics in humans for medical reasons. But should we try for the ultimate mix of human being, artificial parts, and artificial intelligence? Should we try to create a being that is so blended that it's impossible to tell whether it is human or machine?

Some scientists think so. They believe that no matter how complex artificial intelligence gets, robots will never really be able to think like humans. Also, robots will never develop the emotions or instincts that humans rely on in order to behave responsibly. The idea is to take the best of artificial intelligence and body parts, and combine them with the best characteristics of human beings. The idea may sound a little scary, but it could change our entire world.

In science fiction, cyborgs have often been portrayed as threats. Scientists see them as possible allies.

ARTIFICIAL INTELLIGENCE IN THE MOVIES

In a 1999 movie called *Bicentennial Man*, a family purchases a robot named Andrew to do household tasks. Slowly, Andrew begins to develop emotions and over time tries to become legally recognized as "human." The movie raised moral questions about the line between human and machine.

ETHICAL QUESTIONS ABOUT ARTIFICIAL INTELLIGENCE

Artificial intelligence has given us amazing tools that have improved our lives. But is it a cause for concern, as well?

Should we worry that biometrics give the government a lot of very personal information? Is it wrong that scientists use technology to make weapons that kill more efficiently?

Of course, not every issue has to do with our use of the technology. Some people are concerned with the machines that we create. For example, could robots make human workers obsolete? Could artificial intelligence robots start to think on their own? If so, would we have created a population of slaves? These are all **ethical** questions that have come up because of the amazing advances in, and strong possibilities of, artificial intelligence.

Isaac Asimov wrote a series of novels and short stories about "positronic" robots—robots who were conscious of their own existence.

Science fiction writer Isaac Asimov wrote about the future, artificial intelligence, and robots. He came up with The Three Laws of Robotics to make sure humans always stayed in control of machines.

Asimov came up with these laws because the more people learned about artificial intelligence, the more worried they became about what might happen in the future. As we all know, the future has always been a little frightening—but that's what makes it exciting, too.

THE THREE LAWS OF ROBOTICS

1. A robot may not injure a human being or, through inaction, allow a human being to come to harm.

2. A robot must obey orders given it by human beings except where such orders would conflict with the First Law.

3. A robot must protect its own existence as long as such protection does not conflict with the First or Second Law.

ARTIFICIAL INTELLIGENCE IN THE MOVIES

Many writers and moviemakers have explored our fears of the future. The 1968 movie *2001: A Space Odyssey* featured a powerful computer named Hal 9000 that had a mind of its own and tried to take control of a spacecraft. More recently, the *Terminator* movies have explored a future where machines try to take over the world. Luckily, in the movies, human beings always find a way to outwit them.

GLOSSARY

automated A process that works by itself, usually involving machines and computers.

computer revolution A time in the 1980s when home and business computing became affordable and widespread.

database A large collection of organized information.

engineering The science of designing and creating complex products.

ethical Related to personal conduct and acceptable behavior.

interface A device for communicating between two unconnected things.

operating system The program that makes a computer run.

philosopher Someone who studies ideas and theories of existence and life.

programmer Person who creates computer programs.

psychology The science that studies the mind and behavior.

sensor a device that responds to heat, light, or some other stimulus.

simulation An imitation of something real.

terrain The physical features of an area of land.

vacuum tubes Glass tubes filled with gas to control electricity. Used in older televisions and computer monitors.

Find Out More

Books

Engdahl, Sylvia. *Artificial Intelligence*. Farmington Hills, MN: Greenhaven, 2007. This book covers the basics of artificial intelligence and examines the social and ethical issues surrounding it.

Rooney, Anne. *Computers: Faster, Smaller, and Smarter*. Chicago: Heinemann-Raintree, 2006. A look at developing technologies, with glimpses of the future.

Whitby, Blay. *Artificial Intelligence: A Beginner's Guide*. Oxford, England: Oneworld Publications, 2008. A journey into the world of computers, robots, and the mysteries of human thought.

Websites

www.pbs.org/saf/1208/index.html
"The Games Machines Play" is an excellent source for information on recent innovations in artificial intelligence. It includes a young inventors' section and a feature on robot soccer players.

www.sciencedaily.com/news/computers_math/artificial_intelligence
Daily updates and news on new developments in AI. The collection of articles here covers nearly every aspect of the topic.

www.sciencenewsforkids.org
This fascinating site houses articles and informative activities about computers and technology.

INDEX